Catholic Letters

The Epistle of James
The First Epistle of Peter
The Second Epistle of Peter
The Epistle of Jude

STUDY GUIDE

Catherine Upchurch

"Catholic Letters" refers to seven New Testament epistles (James; 1 and 2 Peter; 1, 2, and 3 John; and Jude). They were thought to have had a more universal audience than the Pauline epistles, thus the designation "catholic."

This study focuses on those Catholic Letters found in volume 9 of the Collegeville Bible Commentary.

Little Rock
Scripture Study Program

THE LITURGICAL PRESS

St. John's Abbey
Collegeville, Minnesota 56321

DIOCESE OF LITTLE ROCK
2415 North Tyler Street
P.O. Box 7239, Forest Park Station
LITTLE ROCK, ARKANSAS 72217

Telephone
Area Code 501
664-0340

Office of the Bishop

Dear Friend,

We Catholics have always believed that the Lord is present in his Word, in his sacrament, and through baptism and confirmation in each one of us. In post-Vatican II times, the emphasis upon Jesus in his Word among us has grown and deepened. In many parts of our country, Scripture study programs have become effective instruments for the deepening of our spiritual life.

Some years ago I encouraged our people to embrace God's holy Word. I used the words of Our Lord to St. Augustine, "Take and read." I asked that the Scriptures be prayerfully read. The Little Rock Scripture Study Program provided the way. Out of this program has come an enrichment of our spiritual life and a deeper and closer relationship to the Lord.

The pages of this study guide lay down the challenge to you, the reader. The Word of God can take root in your soul; the Word of God can change your life. The Word of God can make you a saint.

Your friend,

✝ Andrew J. McDonald
Bishop of Little Rock

Sacred Scripture

"The Church has always venerated the divine Scriptures just as she venerates the body of the Lord, since from the table of both the word of God and of the body of Christ she unceasingly receives and offers to the faithful the bread of life, especially in the sacred liturgy. She has always regarded the Scriptures together with sacred tradition as the supreme rule of faith, and will ever do so. For, inspired by God and committed once and for all to writing, they impart the word of God Himself without change, and make the voice of the Holy Spirit resound in the words of the prophets and apostles. Therefore, like the Christian religion itself, all the preaching of the Church must be nourished and ruled by sacred Scripture. For in the sacred books, the Father who is in heaven meets His children with great love and speaks with them; and the force and power in the word of God is so great that it remains the support and energy of the Church, the strength of faith for her sons, the food of the soul, the pure and perennial source of spiritual life."

Vatican II, Dogmatic Constitution on Divine Revelation, no. 21.

INTERPRETATION OF SACRED SCRIPTURE

"Since God speaks in sacred Scripture through men in human fashion, the interpreter of sacred Scripture, in order to see clearly what God wanted to communicate to us, should carefully investigate what meaning the sacred writers really intended, and what God wanted to manifest by means of their words.

"Those who search out the intention of the sacred writers must, among other things, have regard for 'literary forms.' For truth is proposed and expressed in a variety of ways, depending on whether a text is history of one kind or another, or whether its form is that of prophecy, poetry, or some other type of speech. The interpreter must investigate what meaning the sacred writer intended to express and actually expressed in particular circumstances as he used contemporary literary forms in accordance with the situation of his own time and culture. For the correct understanding of what the sacred author wanted to assert, due attention must be paid to the customary and characteristic styles of perceiving, speaking, and narrating which prevailed at the

time of the sacred writer, and to the customs men normally followed
at that period in their everyday dealings with one another."
Vatican II, Dogmatic Constitution on Divine Revelation, no. 12.

Instructions

MATERIALS FOR THE STUDY

This Study Guide: Catholic Letters

Bible: The New American Bible with Revised New Testament
or The New Jerusalem Bible is recommended. Paraphrased edi-
tions are discouraged as they offer little if any help when facing
difficult textual questions. Choose a Bible you feel free to write
in or underline.

Commentary: The Collegeville Bible Commentary: New Testament Series, volume 9, *First Timothy, Second Timothy, Titus,
James, First Peter, Second Peter, Jude* by Jerome H. Neyrey, S.J.
(The Liturgical Press) is used with this study. The abbreviation
for this commentary, CBC-NT volume 9, and the assigned pages
are found at the beginning of each lesson.

ADDITIONAL MATERIALS

Bible Dictionary: *The Dictionary of the Bible* by John L. McKen-
zie (Macmillan) is highly recommended as an additional reference.

Notebook: A notebook may be useful for lecture notes and your
personal reflections.

WEEKLY LESSONS

Lesson 1—Jas 1–2   Lesson 4—1 Pet 3:8–5:14
Lesson 2—Jas 3–5   Lesson 5—2 Pet; Jude
Lesson 3—1 Pet 1:1–3:7

Note: This study does not include questions for First Timothy,
Second Timothy, and Titus, which are not part of the Catholic
Letters.

YOUR DAILY PERSONAL STUDY

The first step is prayer. Open your heart and mind to God. Reading Scripture is an opportunity to listen to God who loves you. Pray that the same Holy Spirit who guided the formation of Scripture will inspire you to correctly understand what you read and empower you to make what you read a part of your life.

The next step is commitment. Daily spiritual food is as necessary as food for the body. This study is divided into daily units. Schedule a regular time and place for your study, as free from distractions as possible. Allow about twenty minutes a day. Make it a daily appointment with God.

As you begin each lesson read the assigned chapters of Scripture found at the beginning of each lesson, the footnotes in your Bible, and then the indicated pages of the commentary. This preparation will give you an overview of the entire lesson and help you to appreciate the context of individual passages.

As you reflect on Scripture, ask yourself these four questions:

1. *What does the Scripture passage say?*
   Read the passage slowly and reflectively. Use your imagination to picture the scene or enter into it.

2. *What does the Scripture passage mean?*
   Read the footnotes and the commentary to help you understand what the sacred writers intended and what God wanted to communicate by means of their words.

3. *What does the Scripture passage mean to me?*
   Meditate on the passage. God's Word is living and powerful. What is God saying to you today? How does the Scripture passage apply to your life today?

4. *What am I going to do about it?*
   Try to discover how God may be challenging you in this passage. An encounter with God contains a challenge to know God's will and follow it more closely in daily life.

THE QUESTIONS ASSIGNED FOR EACH DAY

Read the questions and references for each day. The questions are designed to help you listen to God's Word and to prepare you for the weekly small-group discussion.

Some of the questions can be answered briefly and objectively by referring to the Bible references and the commentary *(What does the passage say?)*. Some will lead you to a better understanding of how the Scriptures apply to the Church, sacraments, and society *(What does the passage mean?)*. Some questions will invite you to consider how God's Word challenges or supports you in your relationships with God and others *(What does the passage mean to me?)*. Finally, the questions will lead you to examine your actions in light of Scripture *(What am I going to do about it?)*.

Write your responses in this study guide or in a notebook to help you clarify and organize your thoughts and feelings.

THE WEEKLY SMALL-GROUP MEETING

The weekly small-group sharing is the heart of the Little Rock Scripture Study Program. Participants gather in small groups to share the results of praying, reading and reflecting on Scripture and on the assigned questions. The goal of the discussion is for group members to be strengthened and nourished individually and as a community through sharing how God's Word speaks to them and affects their daily lives. The daily study questions will guide the discussion; it is not necessary to discuss all the questions.

All members share the responsibility of creating an atmosphere of loving support and trust in the group by respecting the opinions and experiences of others, and by affirming and encouraging one another. The simple shared prayer which begins and ends each small group meeting also helps create the open and trusting environment in which group members can share their faith deeply and grow in the study of God's Word.

A distinctive feature of this program is its emphasis on and trust in God's presence working in and through each member. Sharing responses to God's presence in the Word and in others can bring about remarkable growth and transformation.

THE WRAP-UP LECTURE

The lecture is designed to develop and clarify the themes of the lesson. It is not intended to form the basis for the group discussion. For this reason the lecture is always held at the end of the meeting. If several small groups meet at one time, the large group will gather together in a central location to listen to the lecture.

Lectures may be given by a local speaker. They are also available on audio- or video-cassette.

LESSON 1   Jas 1–2
CBC-NT volume 9, pages 47–55

Day 1

1. a) Identify the three prominent Christians named James in the New Testament. (See Matt 4:21; 10:3; Mark 6:3; Gal 1:19.)
   b) To which of these is the letter most often attributed?

2. a) In what sense can trials be considered "all joy" (1:2)? (See Luke 6:20-23; Rom 5:3-5; 1 Pet 1:6-7; 4:13-14.)
   b) Describe a trial in your own life that you experienced in a positive way.

3. What are some personal and community needs that call for the gift of wisdom (1:5)? (See 1 Kgs 3:9; Prov 3:5-8; Wis 6:12-20; 8:3-8; 1 Cor 2:6-10.)

Day 2

4. How can one determine which "pursuits" are from the Lord (1:11)? (See Matt 6:21, 33.)

5. a) According to James, what is the danger of human desire (1:14)? (See Wis 4:12; Sir 15:11-20; 1 Tim 6:9-10; 2 Tim 2:22.)
   b) What more can you learn about desire in these passages: Psalm 10:17; Proverbs 10:24; Sirach 1:23; Isaiah 32:8?

6. What "perfect gifts" do you recognize in the world around you (1:17)? (See Rom 1:20.)

Day 3

7. What types of behavior might indicate that God's Word has taken root in one's life (1:21-25)? (See Mark 4:20; John 14:23; Col 3:16-17.)

8. "Be doers of the word" (1:22). What parts of God's message are most difficult for you to put into action?

9. a) What are the two elements of pure religion as described by James (1:27)?
   b) How does your parish community exemplify pure religion?

Day 4

10. a) What type of partiality is criticized in 2:1-4? (See 1 Cor 1:26-29.)
    b) How have you been shown partiality in your own life? (See Luke 6:36-37.)

11. What is the source of true wealth (2:5)? (See Matt 6:19-21; Eph 1:18-19; Phil 3:1-5.)

12. What caution is attached to the great command to "love your neighbor as yourself" (2:8-9)? (See Lev 19:18; Matt 22:36-39.)

Day 5

13. a) What does it mean to be "judged by the law of freedom" (2:12-13)? (See 1:25; Rom 8:1-2.)
    b) How does the message of 2:13 affect your life? (See Matt 5:23-24; 6:14-15; 7:1-2.)

14. What ensures a lively faith (2:14-17)? (See Matt 7:18-27; Gal 5:6; 1 John 3:18.)

15. How can the teachings of Paul (Rom 3:28) and the teachings of James be reconciled (2:18-26)?

Day 6

16. What kind of faith do the demons have (2:19)? (See Mark 1:24.)

17. What was the proof of Abraham's faith (2:21-23)? (See Gen 22.)

18. a) Do a person's good works earn salvation? (See Rom 10:17; Gal 5:6; Heb 11:1.)
    b) What did Jesus say about good works? (See Matt 5:16; 7:20-21.)

LESSON 2   Jas 3–5
CBC-NT volume 9, pages 55–64

Day 1

1. What practical insights did you gain from the last discussion or lecture?

2. a) Which of the images of the tongue (ship's rudder, horse's bit, flame) helps you to best uderstand the power of speech (3:3-6)? (See Prov 16:27; Sir 28:12-26.)

   b) What words from others have helped you most? Which have been hurtful?

3. What contradiction does James notice in a Christian's use of his or her tongue (3:9-12)? (See 5:12; Eph 4:29.)

Day 2

4. According to James, what are some of the qualities of an effective teacher (3:1-2, 13-18)?

5. Make a list of what you consider "Wisdom from Above" and another list of "Earthly Wisdom" (3:13-17). (See 1 Cor 2:6-16.)

6. a) In what ways do you "cultivate peace" (3:18) in your home? at your job? (See Matt 5:9; Heb 12:11.)

   b) How has the Church planted seeds of peace and justice in your city, nation, or world?

Day 3

7. Name some life experiences that illustrate the truth of James' teaching about following one's passions (4:1-2). (See Rom 7:22-23.)

8. 4:3 offers one reason we do not always receive what we pray for. What are some other reasons? (See Ps 66:17-18; Matt 7:7-11.)

9. a) Why does James use the term "adulterers" in 4:4?
   b) In what ways could the term describe us today?

Day 4

10. a) How can love of the world be "enmity to God" (4:4)? (See 1 John 2:15-17.)

    b) How can love of the world be a good thing? (See John 3:16.)

11. List the six ways James calls people to return to their faith (4:7-10).

12. When has it been difficult to surrender personal control of your own life to God (4:13-15)? (See Eccl 6:10-12; Matt 6:25-34.)

Day 5

13. a) Why do the Scriptures often connect worldly wealth with injustice (5:1-6)? (See 2:16-17; Luke 16:19-31.)

    b) How can worldly wealth be used as a blessing for others? (See Luke 6:38; Acts 2:44-45.)

14. Describe someone who has been a model of patience in your own life (5:7-10). When has patience helped you in your spiritual journey?

15. Describe a situation when you were impressed by the power of wholesome and positive speech (5:12)? (See Prov 10:20; Matt 5:34-37; Eph 4:25.)

Day 6

16. a) When have you been anointed or witnessed an anointing (5:13-15)?

    b) What are the effects of such anointings?

17. Who may be depending on you for encouragement to overcome sin or return to life in the Church (5:16-20)? (See Gal 6:1-2.)

18. In what ways can your life better express your interior faith, as James encouraged throughout this letter?

LESSON 3   1 Pet 1:1–3:7
CBC-NT volume 9, pages 65–74

Day 1

1. a) Based on your reading of James in the past two lessons, what were some of the difficulties facing the early Church?
   b) Read through 1 Peter and list some of the passages that show similar concerns among Peter's audience.

2. In what ways does the phrase "chosen sojourners" apply to all Christians (1:1)? (See 2:11; Eph 2:19; Heb 11:13-14.)

3. What experiences in your life have reminded you of the "new birth" offered by God (1:3)? (See John 3:5-7; Titus 3:4-6; Jas 1:18.)

Day 2

4. What experiences of suffering have increased the genuineness of your faith (1:6-7)? (See 3:14; 4:13; Rom 5:3-5; Jas 1:2-3.)

5. The author stresses both the freshness of the faith (1:8-9) and its antiquity (1:10-12). Why are both aspects important?

6. Peter encourages his listeners to set their hopes completely on grace and to be obedient to holiness (1:13-15). How would you explain what this means? (See 4:10; Exod 31:13; Lev 19:2; Col 3:12-13; 2 Tim 1:9-10.)

Day 3

7. a) What "futile conduct" does Peter refer to in 1:18? (See 1 Cor 12:2; Eph 4:17-24.)
   b) What conduct today might be considered futile in view of the life offered us by Christ (1:18-19)? (See 2:11.)

8. What is the "imperishable seed" that has led to rebirth (1:23)?

9. What two things are necessary to "grow into salvation" (2:1-2)? (See Jas 1:21.)

Day 4

10. Why would some people prefer to reject the "living stone" rather than build their lives on it (2:4-5)? (See Ps 118:22; Acts 4:11-12.)

11. a) What is the role of the "priesthood" in the following passsages: Leviticus 16:29-34; Hebrews 4:15–5:4; 10:11-12?
    b) In what real ways do we participate in the priesthood of Christ (2:5)?

12. How can awareness of our own stumbling and disobedience make us more effective evangelizers (2:8)?

Day 5

13. a) The early Christians were often alienated from the rest of society. How would the proclamation in 2:9 have affected them? (See Exod 19:5-6.)
    b) What difference does it make in your life to be part of "God's people" and to have "received mercy" (2:10)?

14. What kind of freedom is encouraged in 2:16? (See Rom 8:21; 2 Cor 3:17; Gal 5:13.)

15. a) How can suffering even slavery have value (2:18-21)?
    b) Does the Bible justify slavery? (See Deut 15:12-15; 1 Cor 7:21-24; Gal 3:27-28; Eph 6:5-9.)

Day 6

16. What phrases does the author use to show the real power of Jesus' suffering (2:22-25)? (See Isa 53.)

17. a) According to this letter, what is the purpose of a woman's subordination to her husband in 3:1-2?
    b) How do you feel about the advice offered in 3:1-7? (See 1 Cor 7:3-4; Eph 5:21-30.)

18. Men and women are "joint heirs of the gift of life" (3:7). In what ways is this belief reflected in the changing roles of men and women today? (See Gal 3:27-28.)

LESSON 4   1 Pet 3:8–5:14
CBC-NT volume 9, pages 74–80

Day 1

1. What point from last week's lecture made an impression on you?

2. When has the teaching of 3:9 been most difficult for you to follow? (See Luke 6:27-31.)

3. What life experiences have confirmed your Christian hope (3:15)? (See Ps 39:8; Sir 34:13-14; Rom 5:3-5; Eph 1:18-20.)

Day 2

4. The author of this letter describes Christian belief in a short creedal statement (3:18-22). Write your own statement of belief about Jesus after reading others found in the New Testament. (See Mark 15:39; Acts 2:32-33; Rom 6:8-10; 1 Cor 15:3-5; 1 Tim 3:16.)

5. a) Why is the story of Noah and the flood chosen to prefigure baptism (3:19-20)? (See Gen 6:5-22; 7:6-23; 8:13-22.)
   b) What elements of the baptismal ritual remind you of our share in Jesus' death and resurrection (3:21)? (See Rom 6:3-6; Col 2:12.)

6. a) Peter speaks of one's willingness to suffer as a type of defense against sin (4:1-2). Why would this be true? (See 2:21; Rom 8:18; Rev 2:10.)
   b) What other type of "armor" is spoken of in the New Testament? (See Rom 13:12-14; Eph 6:13-17; 1 Thess 5:8.)

Day 3

7. When have your Christian values come into conflict with the expectations of society (4:3-4)?

8. a) How might unbelievers view the death of Christians (4:6)?
   b) When friends or relatives have died, how has belief in the resurrection made a difference to you?

9. What are some of the positive effects of anticipating final judgment and the "end of all things" (4:6-7)? (See Matt 24:36-44.)

Day 4

10. When have you experienced that "love covers a multitude of sins" (4:8)? (See Prov 10:12; 1 Cor 13:4-7.)

11. a) When has another's hospitality demonstrated true Christian love to you (4:9)? (See Rom 12:13.)
    b) When is it most difficult for you to offer hospitality? (See Heb 13:2.)

12. In your parish what are the gifts most needed to enhance parish life and glorify God (4:10)? (See Rom 12:6-8.)

Day 5

13. From what you know of history, what periods or events would you identify as "a trial by fire" (4:12)? (See 1:6-7; Sir 2:1-6.)

14. In a society like ours, where Christianity is tolerated or accepted, what kinds of suffering might we be asked to endure (4:16)? (See Matt 5:10; Rom 8:16-17.)

15. List several signs that demonstrate God is a "faithful creator" (4:19)? (See Ps 145:13; 1 Cor 1:9.)

Day 6

16. The letter closes with a powerful call to humility.
    a) How are the presbyters to demonstrate humility (5:1-3)?
    b) In what ways can the community also show humility (5:5-6)?

17. Which of your worries are the most difficult to release to Jesus' care (5:7)? Why?

18. Find out what you can about the early Roman persecutions. Why would a greeting from the Church in Rome (5:13) serve as a particular encouragement to other communities?

LESSON 5   2 Pet & Jude
CBC-NT volume 9, pages 81–99

The following twelve questions refer to 2 Peter.

Day 1

1. Why are the Letters of 2 Peter and Jude both considered pseudonymous? (See Introductions in the *Collegeville Bible Commentary*.)

2. Peter expresses the conviction that the faithful will "come to share in the divine nature" (1:4). What does this mean to you? (See John 17:22-23; 1 John 3:2.)

3. a) What qualities and practices are recommended to make one's faith fruitful (1:5-7)?
   b) Describe a situation where these qualities kept you from stumbling (1:10).

Day 2

4. What enduring message do you hope to impart to those who know you (1:13-15)?

5. How does the author prove the reliability of Christian teaching about Jesus' future coming (1:16-21)?

6. How are the false teachers Peter speaks of like the false prophets in Israel's history (2:1)? (See Jer 14:13-14; 23:16-40.)

Day 3

7. a) Why would the author choose examples fron Genesis to demonstrate God's judgment (2:4-10)? (See Jude 5-7.)
   b) Which story, that of Noah or Lot, speaks most powerfully to you of divine judgment and mercy? (See Gen 6:5-9:29; 18:16–19:29.)

8. The following images are found in 2:12-19: irrational animals, eyes full of adultery and insatiable for sin, hearts trained in greed, waterless springs, mists driven by gale, and slaves of corruption (2:12-19). Choose one image and explain how it applies to false teachers.

9. How are those who deny the faith in worse shape than those who have never believed (2:21-22)? (See Ezek 3:20; Gal 4:8-9.)

Day 4

10. a) When was the last time you heard "scoffing" about Christian beliefs (3:3)? What was the belief being disputed?
    b) Can you think of a time when your faith was ridiculed? How did you respond?

11. What is the cause for God's patience in returning (3:9)? (See 1 Tim 2:3-4.)

12. Why does this letter focus on the certainty of Christ's coming rather than the time of his coming (3:10-16)? (See Mark 13:32-33; Rev 21:1-4.)

The remaining questions refer to the Letter of Jude.

Day 5

13. The Letter of Jude addresses the Church as "those who are kept safe for Jesus Christ" (1). How does your parish promote and guard the message of Christ?

14. Jude refers to false teachers as "dreamers" (8). What examples does the author use to remind them of the reality of divine judgment (5-11)? (See Gen 4:8-16; Num 16:1-35; 31:16.)

15. a) What actions are believers called to in the face of false teaching (22-23)?
    b) What can you do when concerned about the spiritual life of those you love?

Day 6

16. What might make an individual or a community vulnerable to the false teaching spoken of in 2 Peter and Jude?

17. What universal concerns of the Church have been addressed throughout this study?

18. In what practical ways would you like to respond to the universal message of these letters?

NOTES